Is it transparent or opaque?

Susan Hughes

Crabtree Publishing Company

www.crabtreebooks.com

MAI 863 7912

What's the Matter?

Author: Susan Hughes
Publishing plan research and development:
   Sean Charlebois, Reagan Miller
   Crabtree Publishing Company
Project development: Clarity Content Services
Project management: Karen Iversen
Project coordinator: Kathy Middleton
Editors: Susan Hughes, Kathy Middleton
Copy editor: Dimitra Chronopoulos
Proofreader: Reagan Miller
Design: First Image
Photo research: Linda Tanaka
Prepress technician: Katherine Berti
Print and production coordinator: Katherine Berti

Photographs:
p1 Lifesize/Thinkstock; p4 Johan Swanepoel/shutterstock;
p5 Andresr/shutterstock; p6 Willecole/dreamstime.com; p7
Hemera/Thinkstock; p8 shutterstock; p9 shutterstock; p10 Villedieu
Christophe/shutterstock; p11 top right essenin quijada/iStock, Jorg
Hackemann/shutterstock; p12 iStockphoto/Thinkstock; p13 top left
Fuse/Thinkstock, snake3d/shutterstock; p14 Frances A. Miller/
shutterstock; p15 iStockphoto/Thinkstock; p16 Valentina R./
shutterstock; p17 top aspen rock/shutterstock, mrsnstudio/
shutterstock; p18 David Tanaka; p19 fuyu liu/shutterstock; p21
Angela Sorrentino/iStock; p22 top right Gilmanshin/shutterstock,
Hemera/Thinkstock; cover shutterstock

Library and Archives Canada Cataloguing in Publication

Hughes, Susan, 1960-
   Is it transparent or opaque? / Susan Hughes.

(What's the matter?)
Includes index.
Issued also in electronic formats.
ISBN 978-0-7787-2052-2 (bound).--ISBN 978-0-7787-2059-1 (pbk.)

   1. Transparency--Juvenile literature. 2. Opacity (Optics)--
Juvenile literature. 3. Materials--Optical properties--Juvenile
literature. 4. Matter--Properties--Juvenile literature.
I. Title. II. Series: What's the matter? (St. Catharines, Ont.)

TA418.62.H84 2012   j620.1'1295   C2012-900295-X

Library of Congress Cataloging-in-Publication Data

Hughes, Susan, 1960-
Is it transparent or opaque? / Susan Hughes.
p. cm. -- (What's the matter?)
Includes index.
ISBN 978-0-7787-2052-2 (reinforced library binding : alk. paper) --
ISBN 978-0-7787-2059-1 (pbk. : alk. paper) -- ISBN 978-1-4271-7950-0
(electronic pdf) -- ISBN 978-1-4271-8065-0 (electronic html)
1. Transparency--Juvenile literature. 2. Opacity (Optics)--Juvenile literature.
3. Matter--Properties--Juvenile literature. I. Title.

QC173.36.H83 2012
535'.3--dc23

2012000121

Crabtree Publishing Company

www.crabtreebooks.com   1-800-387-7650

Printed in the U.S.A./032012/CJ20120215

Published in Canada
Crabtree Publishing
616 Welland Ave.
St. Catharines, ON
L2M 5V6

Published in the United States
Crabtree Publishing
PMB 59051
350 Fifth Avenue, 59th Floor
New York, New York 10118

Published in the United Kingdom
Crabtree Publishing
Maritime House
Basin Road North, Hove
BN41 1WR

Published in Australia
Crabtree Publishing
3 Charles Street
Coburg North
VIC 3058

What is in this book?

What is matter?

All objects are made of **matter**.

Matter takes up space.

Matter has **mass**.

Mass is the amount of material in an object.

Everything is made
of matter—even you!

What are properties?

Matter has **properties**.

Properties describe how something looks, feels, tastes, smells, or sounds.

We can look at something to see if it is big or small.

Size is a property.

We can feel something
to see if it is rough or smooth.

Texture, or how something feels,
is a property, too.

Can we see through it?

Some materials let light pass through them and others do not. This is a property of the material.

If light can pass through a material, then we can see through it.

Materials we can see through are called **transparent**.

8

A magnifying glass is transparent.

So are eyeglasses and windows.

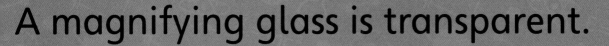

Why do we need to see through some objects?

What is opaque?

Some materials do not let any light pass through.

We cannot see through them.

Materials we cannot see through are called **opaque**.

This door is opaque.

These curtains are opaque.

This sleep mask
is opaque.

What happens to a room
when you close the curtains?
Why is it important for some
objects to be opaque?

11

What is translucent?

Some things let some light shine through.

We can see through them a little.

These materials are called **translucent**.

Tissue paper is translucent.

12

This jelly is translucent.

These balloons are translucent.

Three in one!

Look at this stained-glass window.

It is made of pieces of glass stuck together.

Some glass is clear, and some is colored.

The glass pieces are held in place by metal strips of lead.

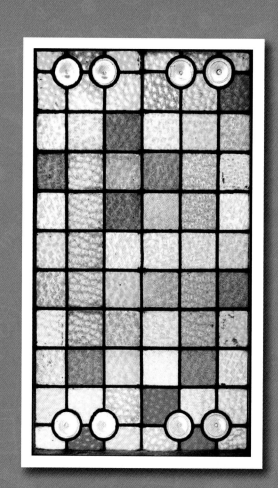

Which materials in this stained-glass window are transparent, translucent, or opaque?

15

Which property is it?

Light cannot pass through this apple.

The apple is opaque.

Light can shine through this glass pitcher. The glass pitcher is transparent.

Some light can shine through the candies shown below.

The gummies are translucent.

Shine a flashlight on some other objects to see if light passes through them.

Experiment with bubbles

Mix liquid soap with water.

Add a small amount of sugar.

Pour the bubble mix into a flat pan.

Make a wand with a pipe cleaner.

Dip and blow!

Are the bubbles transparent or opaque?

Are the bubbles translucent?

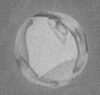

What clues helped you decide which property the bubbles have?

Shadow shapes

When light cannot pass through an object, a **shadow** forms. A shadow is a dark area on a surface near the object.

An opaque object makes a shadow. It blocks light from passing through.

A translucent object also makes a shadow. It can block some light.

A tranparent object does not make a shadow. It cannot block light.

You can use your hands to make shapes like the one in this picture.

Turn on one light in a dark room.

Hold your hands up between the light and a wall.

Moves your hands in different ways.

What shadow shapes can you make?

21

Guess the shape

A shadow looks like the shape of the object that forms it.

This picture shows a palm tree and the shadow it makes.

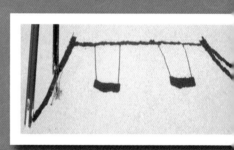

Guess what objects are making the shadows shown on the right.

Words to know and Index

Notes for adults

Objectives

- to introduce children to the difference between transparent, opaque, and translucent objects
- to learn about how people use these objects in everyday life

Prerequisite

Have the children read other books in the series, such as *Is it smooth or rough?*, or *Is it magnetic or nonmagnetic?* before reading *Is it transparent or opaque?* Introducing them to the concepts of matter via the other books in the series will help familiarize them with the initial concepts in this book.

Questions before reading *Is it transparent or opaque?*

"What are some things you can see through? What are some things that you cannot see through?"

"What materials would you use to wrap a birthday gift for a friend? Why?"

"Why would you want a flashlight bulb to be made of a material you can see through?"

"Why would you want your sunglasses to be made of a material that blocks out a bit of light?"

Discussion

Read the book to the children. Discuss with the children some of the main concepts in the book, such as transparent, translucent, and opaque.

Discuss the many reasons why people choose to use transparent or opaque materials. You may need to provide some examples, such as a skylight in the roof of a house, a sunroof in a car, the walls in a greenhouse or a solarium, the glass on the bottom of a glass-bottomed boat, the walls of a photographer's "dark room," the black curtain in a theater, and so on.

Extension

Encourage the children to use a flashlight to check whether several materials or objects are transparent, translucent, or opaque. Have them make a prediction first. Provide a large piece of chart paper with the three categories listed. Ask the children to list or draw their results in the appropriate column after they test each material or object.